DINNERTIME
for Animals

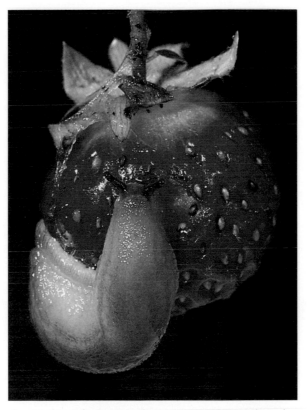

A garden slug munches a strawberry lunch.

by Jane R. McCauley

BOOKS FOR YOUNG EXPLORERS
NATIONAL GEOGRAPHIC SOCIETY

Mother mammals feed their young.

On a thick bed of grass, a mother grizzly bear is nursing her cubs. For several months the cubs drink their mother's milk. They follow her when she hunts for food, for one day they will be on their own.

A young kangaroo, or joey, stays snug inside its mother's pouch. As she stoops to eat grass, the joey is close enough to nibble some, too. It needs more food than just its mother's milk.

Some birds bring food to their young.

Cheep! Cheep! A fairy tern chick signals its parents that it is hungry. One parent soon brings a little fish.

A young pelican pokes its bill into its parent's throat to find a meal.

The father and mother pelican scoop fish from the water with their pouches. They swallow the fish whole or carry them back to the young in their bills.

LESSER LONG-TONGUED BAT

PASSION VINE BUTTERFLY

Many kinds of animals feed on plants.

This bat is drinking nectar from a blossom. The bat lives in a rain forest and looks for food at night.

By day, a butterfly moves among its favorite flowers. It sucks nectar through its proboscis, a part of its mouth that acts as a straw.

In the treetops of a rain forest, capuchin monkeys tear into papaya fruit. With their skillful hands, these monkeys find many things to eat as they move through the forest. They eat leaves, insects, eggs, and small birds and mammals, as well as fruit.

WHITE-FACED CAPUCHIN (kuh-PYOO-shun) MONKEYS

Plant-eaters

On a grassy plain, a herd of bison grazes in the sunshine. Enough grass is growing to feed these bison for many months. A ground squirrel scampers all over to find nuts and seeds in the fall. It stuffs one after another into its cheek pouches. It will hide them away to eat later.

Some animals store food.

With its sharp bill, an acorn woodpecker chips holes in the bark of a tree. The bird puts acorns away to eat in winter. How many acorns do you count? A hungry squirrel may steal some of them.

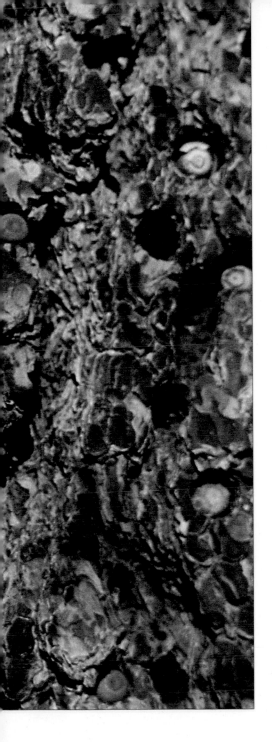

Harvester ants save seeds
in storerooms they dig under the
ground. This ant is carrying
home a fluffy seed. Through
tunnels they make, the ants
move from room to room, taking
care of their piles of seeds.

Others that store

This camel has saved a lot of food.
It is stored as fat inside the humps.
When food is scarce, the camel uses
the fat for energy. The humps slowly
shrink and flop over as fat is used.

As it sips nectar from a flower,
a honeybee collects pollen, too.
It packs the yellow pollen in pouches
on its rear legs to use as food later.
Do you know what bees make from
the nectar they take to their hive?
They make honey, which we eat, too.

It's always dinnertime for some animals.

SEA ANEMONES (uh-NEM-uh-neez)

Undersea animals that look like plants just sit and wait for food. The living parts of coral branches, called polyps, sift food from the water.
A sea anemone has tentacles that sting small sea animals and pull them to its mouth.

Some animals hunt others to eat.

Two dingoes, Australian dogs that live wild, move carefully to corner a lizard called a goanna. The goanna puffs up and stands up tall to make itself look bigger.

Hunters

Sharp eyesight helps a sea eagle swoop down and snatch a fish for breakfast.

On the grassland, speedy legs help a cheetah cub outrun
a young springbok. A springbok, a kind of antelope, runs swiftly.
But cheetahs are the fastest of all land mammals over short
distances. Will the springbok escape? Probably it will not.

Special body parts help animals hunt.

A chameleon goes after a butterfly. Lightning fast, it shoots its tongue out. Then back comes the tongue with the butterfly stuck to the tip. YUMMM!

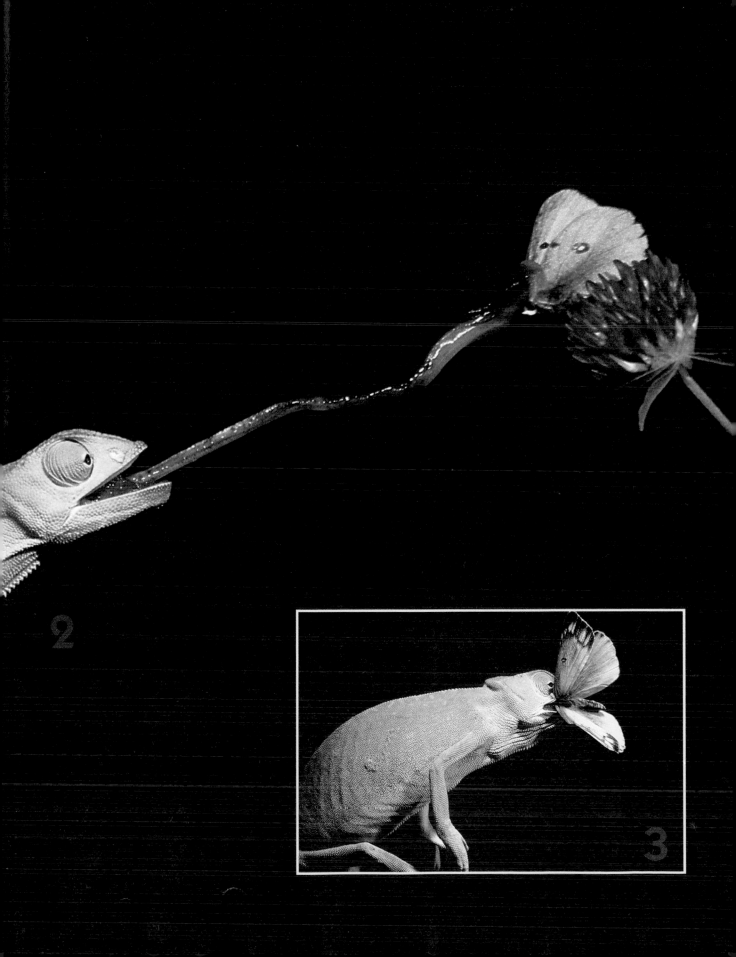

2

3

Help from claws and bills

A lobster holds a herring with its claws. The small teeth
in its right claw help the lobster tear away bites to eat.
A bill shaped like a long spoon helps the roseate spoonbill
gather food in the water. The bird swishes its open bill from side
to side until it feels a fish inside. Then it clamps its mouth shut.

Some animals use tools.

Floating on its back, a sea otter bangs a clam against a rock resting on its belly. Again and again, the otter bangs the shell until it cracks open.

Chimpanzees fish for termites by poking grass or twigs into a nest. With their lips, they pick off termites that bite the twigs.

Finding food sometimes helps others.

What is the oxpecker doing on the Cape buffalo's nose?
It may be finding moisture there. This kind of bird often
sits on a buffalo and cleans its hide by eating ticks
and other pests that bother the huge animal.
In this way, the bird and the buffalo help each other.

Tiny fish called neon gobies get food by cleaning bigger fish.
A stoplight parrotfish keeps very still while the gobies work.
They will even clean inside the parrotfish's mouth.
After a while, other fish will swim by for a cleaning.

Some animals are picky eaters.

In its wild home in China, the giant panda
crunches on little else but bamboo.
When bamboo is scarce, pandas may starve.
The monarch caterpillar prefers to nibble the
leaves of the milkweed plant. Before long,
the caterpillar will turn into a beautiful butterfly.

These animals, like some people, are picky
about what they eat. Other animals find food
almost anywhere. Each kind of animal
has its own menu at dinnertime.

Others will eat almost anything.

Sea gulls feast at a landfill, where people have dumped wastes. Tomatoes growing in a garden taste good to an opossum, but this animal might even find its dinner in your garbage can.

Published by
The National Geographic Society, Washington, D.C.
Gilbert M. Grosvenor, *President and Chairman of the Board*
Michela A. English, *Senior Vice President*
Robert L. Breeden, *Executive Adviser to the President for Publications and Educational Media*

Prepared by
The Book Division
William R. Gray, *Director*
Margery G. Dunn, *Senior Editor*

Staff for this book
Jane H. Buxton, *Managing Editor*
Thomas B. Powell III, *Illustrations Editor*
Suez B. Kehl, *Art Director*
Elizabeth W. Fisher, Ann Nottingham Kelsall, *Researchers*
Artemis S. Lampathakis, *Illustrations Assistant*
Karen F. Edwards, Sandra F. Lotterman, Teresita Cóquia Sison, Marilyn J. Williams, *Staff Assistants*

Engraving, Printing, and Product Manufacture
George V. White, *Director,* and Vincent P. Ryan, *Manager, Manufacturing and Quality Management*
Heather Guwang, *Production Project Manager*
Lewis R. Bassford, Richard S. Wain, *Production*

Consultants
James M. Dietz, David Inouye, University of Maryland; Craig Phillips, Biologist; George E. Watson, St. Albans School, Washington, D.C., *Scientific Consultants*
Susan Altemus, *Educational Consultant*
Lynda Bush, *Reading Consultant*

Illustrations Credits

Dwight R. Kuhn (cover, 1, 20-21 all, 29); W. Perry Conway / TOM STACK & ASSOCIATES (2); John Cancalosi (3); Frans Lanting / MINDEN PICTURES (4 both); Alan & Sandy Carey (5); Merlin D. Tuttle / BAT CONSERVATION INTERNATIONAL (6 upper); Michael Fogden (6 lower); ©Jack Swenson (7); Kent & Donna Dannen (8 inset); Diana L. Stratton / TOM STACK & ASSOCIATES (8-9); Kathy Watkins / IMAGES OF NATURE (10-11); Ross E. Hutchins (11 both); Len Rue, Jr. / RUE ENTERPRISES (12-13); David P. Maitland / AUSCAPE INTERNATIONAL (13); Jett Britnell / DRK PHOTO (14 inset); ANIMALS ANIMALS / Mickey Gibson (14-15); Jean-Paul Ferrero / AUSCAPE INTERNATIONAL (16-17); Charles G. Summers, Jr. / TOM STACK & ASSOCIATES (18); Dieter & Mary Plage / BRUCE COLEMAN INC. (18-19); Breck P. Kent (22, 28, 32); E.R. Degginger (23); Tom & Pat Leeson (24); Hugo Van Lawick (24-25); Fred Bavendam / PETER ARNOLD, INC. (26); Stephen J. Krasemann / DRK PHOTO (27); Gay Bumgarner (30); Ray Pfortner / PETER ARNOLD, INC. (30-31).

Library of Congress ☭ Data
McCauley, Jane R., 1947-
  Dinnertime for Animals / by Jane R. McCauley.
  p. cm. — (Books for young explorers)
  Includes bibliographical references.
  Summary: Explains how different animals living in the wild have divergent diets, eating habits, and methods of gathering food for survival.
  ISBN 0-87044-844-7 (regular edition) — ISBN 0-87044-849-8 (library edition)
  1. Animals—Food—Juvenile literature. [1. Animals—Food habits.]
I. Title. II. Series.
QL756.5.M37 1991
591.53—dc20   91-12111
                                                  ☭
                                                  AC

Blackberries ripening in the summer bring a hungry box turtle out of its shell.

Cover: The striped bill of a puffin holds a good catch of fish scooped from the sea.

MORE ABOUT DINNERTIME for Animals

Life for all animals revolves around their ability to find food. Night and day, on land and in the water, animals are busily searching for meals for themselves and for their young.

Scientists classify animals as plant-eaters (herbivores), meat-eaters (carnivores), or those that feed on both plants and animals (omnivores). By looking through this book, you can find examples of all three kinds.

Though classified as carnivores, grizzly bears (2)* are omnivorous. They will eat insects, berries, roots, and fish—whatever is in season— as well as small mammals and carrion. The grizzlies' first food— like that of all other mammals—is their mother's milk. Cubs learn to find other foods by following their mother as she roams. The mother can nurse them longer than usual if food is scarce. Bears, like many other animals, store food as fat. Over the summer, bears feed voraciously and build up fat reserves they will need to sustain them in the winter.

Fairy terns (4) grow up quickly. For a while, though, their parents work constantly, bringing them small fish to eat. The chick hatches from an egg balanced on a branch, in the fork of a tree, or sometimes atop a woodpile.

In the ocean, minute plants and animals called plankton help sustain much of the life there. Corals (14-15) collect the drifting plankton on their feathery branches, which sway continuously with the ocean currents. Flower-like sea anem-

ALAN & SANDY CAREY

Mare and foal enjoy a leisurely lunch by the hay wagon in a neat Montana barnyard. Unlike their feral relatives, which roam wild rangelands in search of food, these horses receive help from human hands.

ones, creatures that remain fixed to one place like coral, sting prey with their tentacles. The victim is then trapped as the tentacles close around it.

Slow-moving scavengers of the ocean bottom, lobsters (22) feed on live prey or decaying organisms, as well as seaweed and bits of bone and shell. A lobster crushes its prey with the blunt teeth on one claw. With the sharper, finer teeth on the other claw, it breaks off small pieces and brings them to its mouth. Like humans, lobsters may be either right-handed or left-handed.

The agile sea otter (24) favors shellfish. This furry creature uses a tool to get at its food. Diving underwater, an otter will bring up a

clam or abalone along with a rock. The otter flips over, holding the rock on its belly, and smashes the clam against the rock until the shell cracks open. After eating, the fastidious otter rolls over, washing bits of food from its fur.

Many animals rely on others for their food. Slender gobies (26) get their meals by cleaning bigger fish. Gobies tend to keep to certain areas on coral reefs. Their brilliant coloration and wavy motions attract fish to them.

In another cooperative relationship, oxpeckers (27), or tick birds, pick off ticks and other parasites from the hide of large animals such as Africa's Cape buffalo. Sometimes two or three oxpeckers hitchhike on a buffalo's back. If the birds

* Numbers in parentheses refer to pages in *Dinnertime for Animals*.

Finches bask in the sunshine and wait their turn to eat sunflower seeds thoughtfully provided for them in a backyard feeder.

are alarmed, they chirp suddenly and fly away. Then the buffalo becomes alert to danger.

Some animals are aided in their quest for food by specialized skills or body parts. The cheetah (18), for example, uses its speed in chasing prey. On its long, muscular legs, it dashes as fast as 60 miles an hour when chasing springboks or hares. The cheetah is the fastest land mammal over short distances.

A chameleon (20-21) hunts with its sticky tongue, which, when fully extended, is longer than the rest of its body. Strong muscles on the sides enable the chameleon to thrust its tongue way out. Prey sticks to the bulb at the tip.

Many chameleons live in rain forests, where great numbers of plant-eaters such as the lesser long-tongued bat (6) find a home. This bat stays aloft while drinking nectar by fluttering its short, broad

wings. Pollen sticks to its fur and is spread from flower to flower as the bat flies about at night. Animals such as this are losing their homes and food supply as rain forests rapidly disappear.

Dwindling food supply also threatens the giant panda of China (28). Pandas face loss of habitat as people encroach on their remote, mountainous territory. In addition, the giant pandas' primary food source—bamboo—may suddenly disappear. On the rare occasions when bamboo flowers, the stalks of one species all die at the same time. It takes several years for enough new plants to grow to replenish the pandas' food supply, and some pandas starve during this phase of the growth cycle.

The monarch caterpillar (29) depends on the milkweed plant for food and, indirectly, for protection. The sap of the milkweed is poisonous to other animals, so the butterflies that develop from those caterpillars are themselves poisonous if eaten. Chickadees and warblers never eat monarch butterflies. Jays, curiously, seem to know to discard the wings—the most poisonous part—but they can eat the rest safely.

In contrast to picky eaters, there are animals that will munch on almost anything. Box turtles (32) and opossums (30) poke around in gardens, dining on whatever vegetables or berries they see. Turtles also eat slugs. Refuse in landfills provides meals for thousands of sea gulls (30-31).

Landfills, city parks, even your own backyard are good places for you and your child to observe the fascinating eating habits of animals. Here are some other ways to learn about animals' dinnertimes:

● Visit the zoo. Call ahead to find out the feeding times. With a notepad and pencil, you can make a journal of your observations. Watch different kinds of animals as they eat. What body parts do they use? Are they carnivores, herbivores, or omnivores?

● If you have a pet, notice its eating habits. How do they compare with those of the wild animals described in this book or with those you see at the zoo?

● Draw a picture of the ocean floor or a rain forest. Look back through the book and draw animals eating in these places. For example, you could draw a butterfly sipping from a flower, or a sea anemone with its tentacles closing around a fish.

● One of the best ways to begin your explorations is to hang an inexpensive bird feeder at home. Encourage your children to observe the birds that visit it. At the library you can find books to help identify them. Remind your children never to disturb animals while they are feeding.

ADDITIONAL READING

The Amazing Things Animals Do, by Susan McGrath. (Washington, D.C., National Geographic Society, 1989). Ages 8-12.

Animal Behavior, An Evolutionary Approach, by John Alcock. (Sunderland, Mass., Sinauer Associates, Inc., 1988). Family reference.

Book of Mammals, 2 vols. (Washington, D.C., National Geographic Society, 1981). Ages 8 and up.

The Trials of Life, by David Attenborough. (Boston, Little, Brown and Company, 1990). Family reference.